For Your Wedding

ACCESSORIES

For Your Wedding

ACCESSORIES

Tracy Guth

Principal photography by Lyn Hughes

FRIEDMAN/FAIRFAX
PUBLISHERS

A FRIEDMAN/FAIRFAX BOOK
Friedman/Fairfax Publishers
15 West 26 Street
New York, NY 10010
Telephone (212) 685-6610
Fax (212) 685-1307
Please visit our website: www.metrobooks.com

Library of Congress Cataloging-in-Publication Data

Guth, Tracy.
    Accessories / Tracy Guth.
        p. cm. — (For your wedding)
    Includes bibliographical references and index.
    ISBN 1-56799-931-X
        1. Wedding costume. 2. Dress acessories. I. Title. II. Series.

TT633.G877 2000
392.5′4—dc21
                                                                99-053876

Editor: Ann Kirby
Art Director: Jeff Batzli
Designer: Jennifer O'Connor
Photography Editor: Wendy Missan
Production: Richela Fabian and Camille Lee

Color separations by Colourscan Overseas Co Pte Ltd
Printed in Hong Kong by C&C Offset Printing Co., Ltd.

1 3 5 7 9 10 8 6 4 2

Distributed by Sterling Publishing Co., Inc.
387 Park Avenue South
New York, NY 10016-8810
Orders and customer service (800) 367-9692
Fax: (800) 542-7567
E-mail: custservice@sterlingpub.com
Website: www.sterlingpublishing.com

Cover photograph: ©Lyn Hughes

CONTENTS

INTRODUCTION

You probably heard it from your mother on prom night: accessories make the outfit. This is no less true when it comes to your wedding day. Of course, your gown is a vision of gorgeousness in its own right; bridal accessories will only enhance your look, and, just as important, personalize it. Although most brides wear a white dress on their big day, none of them will look exactly the way you do: the endless combinations of each gown with different headpieces, veils, purses, and shoes provide countless possibilities for a truly unique look.

The same dress can look dramatically different depending on the accessories a bride chooses to wear. For example, a simple white sheath dress paired with a delicate silver tiara, silver sandals, and a ruby pendant creates quite a different impression than the same dress worn with full, floor-length veiling, classic white opera gloves, and a string of pearls. And consider the drama a scarlet cape would add to a full ball gown for a December wedding.

From your head (veil, headpiece) to your toes (a fabulous pair of shoes) and everywhere in between (jewelry, gloves, a wrap, a purse) and underneath (the perfect lingerie), there are plenty of wedding-day accessory decisions to make. Go with your instinct and trust your personal style. But don't overdo it—a few well-chosen pieces will finish your look beautifully. Remember, nothing's mandatory, and nothing is prohibited. If you're uncomfortable wearing gloves or carrying a purse—or even with wearing a veil—there's no rule that says you must. On the contrary, if you have always dreamed of opera-length gloves or a glittering crown of rhinestones, there are few times in your life that these stunning pieces will be more appropriate than on your wedding day.

Keep in mind that you may not have to plan all your accessories yourself. There's a wonderful tradition derived from an Old English rhyme:

Something old,

Something new,

Something borrowed,

Something blue . . .

And a silver sixpence in her shoe.

These meaningful objects are usually presented to you by close relatives and friends, to bring you luck and prosperity in your new marriage. Something old

represents continuity, a link with the past; you could don the headpiece your great-grandmother wore, or wear an heirloom pearl necklace. Something new stands for hope for the future; a gift of silk stockings from your mother or a pretty purse from your maid of honor would be perfect. Something borrowed usually comes from a happily married female relative or friend and is offered for luck. Your aunt might lend those earrings of hers that you so love, or your best friend might present you with the tiara she wore on her own blissful wedding day. Something blue symbolizes loyalty, prosperity, and love. Many brides wear blue garters, but you may consider a powder-blue bra, gloves—or simply painting your toenails in a

THESE ANTIQUE CLIP-ON EARRINGS ECHO THE CURVY SPIRALS OF THE COUPLE'S MONOGRAMMED INVITATION. NO, YOU DON'T HAVE TO BE COORDINATED DOWN TO THAT LEVEL OF DETAIL, BUT THIS IS A WONDERFUL EXAMPLE OF HOW INSPIRATION CAN BE FOUND EVERYWHERE—EVEN IN YOUR STATIONERY.

shimmering shade of aquamarine. That silver sixpence in your shoe represents fortune, so tuck a dime under your heel before you walk down the aisle!

Deciding on your wedding-day accessories can be a lot of fun, especially because you'll likely be choosing most of them when the majority of your big wedding-day decisions having already been made. These finishing touches can be found at bridal stores, antique shops, even in the closets of your closest friends and family.

RIGHT: THIS BEAUTIFUL HEADBAND FEATURES LAYERS OF EMBROIDERED PATTERNS AND COLORS. SILVER BLUE, GOLD, AND GREEN MELD WITH BRIDAL IVORY TO CREATE A UNIQUE HEADPIECE THAT WILL BE A MAJOR TOPIC OF CONVERSATION—AND IT'S EASY TO WEAR, WITH OR WITHOUT A VEIL.

OPPOSITE: ALONG WITH YOUR RING PILLOW, CAKE KNIFE, UNITY CANDLE, AND OTHER ACCESSORIES, THE GARTER IS A WONDERFUL WEDDING-DAY KEEPSAKE. YOU MIGHT EVEN CHOOSE TO KEEP YOURS FOR YOUR OWN DAUGHTER TO WEAR SOMEDAY AT HER OWN WEDDING, OR FOR YOUR SON TO GIVE TO HIS BRIDE.

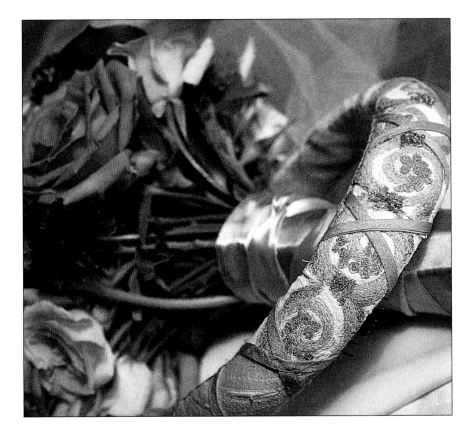

OPPOSITE: THE RIBBON DETAILS CRISSCROSSING THE TOES OF THESE SHOES ARE ECHOED IN THE SEXY STRAPS. IF YOU'RE NOT USUALLY A HIGH-HEEL PERSON, CONSIDER A SANDAL WITH GOOD SUPPORT, LIKE THESE. YOU MIGHT BE WEAK IN THE KNEES ON YOUR WEDDING DAY, BUT DON'T GO WEAK IN THE ANKLES, TOO!

LEFT: YOU'LL FIND A PERFECTLY PERT PILLBOX HAT THE IDEAL ACCESSORY FOR THE RIGHT GOWN. THINK SIMPLE LINES, MINIMAL EMBELLISHMENT, AND THREE-QUARTER SLEEVES —OR EVEN A LITTLE WHITE SUIT. A FAVORITE STYLE OF JACKIE KENNEDY AND AUDREY HEPBURN, THIS SOPHISTICATED PILLBOX FEATURES A SMALL, PRETTY BOW. A WIDE-NET FACE VEIL IS A SMART FINISHING TOUCH.

CHAPTER ONE

VEILS AND HEADPIECES

PAGE 14: PEEK THROUGH THIS BRIDE'S ELBOW-LENGTH LAYERS OF ORGANZA AND YOU'LL SEE TINY SILK FLOWERS ENSCONCED IN HER HAIR. THESE DETAILS ADD A TOUCH OF ROMANCE TO HER SIMPLE SILK DRESS, WITH ITS DRAMATIC PLUNGING BACK.

OPPOSITE: THIS BRIDE HAS PUT TOGETHER THE PERFECT HEADPIECE LOOK—A LONG BUT SIMPLE VEIL IS ATTACHED AT THE CROWN OF HER HEAD, WITH HER SHORT HAIR TEASED AROUND IT TO HOLD IT IN PLACE. A SIMPLE BAND OF SATIN TRIM ALONG ITS EDGE ECHOES THE HEM OF HER CLASSIC BALL GOWN.

LEFT: TIERS OF TULLE CASCADE DOWN FROM THE TOP OF THIS BRIDE'S HEAD WITH THIS CLASSIC WATERFALL VEIL. THIS FULL, STUNNING VEIL PERFECTLY COMPLEMENTS A SIMPLE DRESS, BE IT A TRADITIONAL BALL GOWN OR AN ULTRA-MODERN SHEATH.

*T*raditionally, brides were veiled as a sign of purity, but veils also served as a protective shield. In ancient times, brides often wore red veils to scare away evil spirits, or yellow to honor Hymen, the ancient Greek god of marriage. During the days of arranged marriages, the veiled bride didn't actually lay eyes on her groom—nor did he get a glimpse of her—until they were already wed! For today's bride, the veil may be worn for its traditional symbolism or because the bride simply wants to be veiled. Some women choose not to wear one, opting to walk into marriage with an uncovered head, or they might opt for a wreath of fresh flowers. Still, many modern

RIGHT: DELICATE SILK ROSES RESEMBLE THE REAL THING AND LOOK GORGEOUS PAIRED WITH A SIMPLE TULLE VEIL. FLORAL HEADPIECES MAY ECHO THE DETAILS ON A BRIDE'S DRESS, OR MIMIC THE BLOOMS SHE CHOOSES TO CARRY IN HER BOUQUET.

OPPOSITE: YOUR DRESS IS SIMPLE AND UNADORNED, JUST THE WAY YOU WANTED IT, BUT YOU'D LIKE TO ADD SOME TEXTURE. CHOOSE A VEIL WITH ELABORATE FLORAL LACE DETAILS WOVEN THROUGH IT. THE POSSIBLE PATTERNS ARE LIMITLESS, AND THIS IS ALSO A WONDERFUL WAY TO INTRODUCE SOME COLOR INTO YOUR ENSEMBLE.

brides view their veil and headpiece as a stylish statement. And that's easy to do, because there are so many options. Here are some examples of the many different types of hair ornaments:

Tiaras: Probably the most popular option, tiaras today are smaller and more delicate than they used to be, made of pretty metals (silver, gold, bronze, or a combination) and adorned with colorful gems (white, blue, pink, or purple rhinestones; semiprecious stones like amethyst or citrine), beads, and crystals. High, elaborate crowns are available, but most brides opt for something lower and smaller, more like a three-dimensional headband. Tiaras can be worn alone or with veiling attached, and they look gorgeous with long or short hair.

(continued on page 23)

CONSIDER HAVING YOUR
OWN HAIR—OR NATURAL-
LOOKING EXTENSIONS—
FASHIONED INTO AN
ORNATE COIFFURE IN LIEU
OF A HEADPIECE. THIS
BRIDE'S HAIR IS BRAIDED
AND WRAPPED INTO A
ROMANTIC ELIZABETHAN
STYLE, THEN EMBELLISHED
WITH SPARKLING PINS.

A SLIM SHEATH DRESS TAKES
ON AN ETHEREAL FEEL WHEN
PAIRED WITH CHAPEL-LENGTH
WATERFALL VEILING. THE LONG
LAYERS OF ORGANZA EXTEND
WELL PAST THE HEM OF THE
DRESS, DOUBLING AS A TRAIN.
THIS BRIDE ALSO WEARS AN
ELBOW-LENGTH BLUSHER VEIL,
TO BE PLACED OVER HER FACE
FOR THE CEREMONY.

OPPOSITE: A COMB IS OFTEN USED TO ATTACH A VEIL TO LONG, THICK HAIR BECAUSE IT CAN BE SECURED EASILY INTO A SCULPTED UPDO OR IN LAYERS OF THICK, CURLY TRESSES. THIS BRIDE CHOSE A SIMPLE LENGTH OF ORGANZA AND JUST A FEW BLOOMS TO ACCENT HER LUSTROUS LOCKS.

LEFT: THIS ELABORATE HEADPIECE RESEMBLES FINE PORCELAIN. DELICATE ROSE SHAPES ARE EMBELLISHED WITH TINY SPRAYS OF BEADS, LIKE BABY'S BREATH. A SIMPLE TULLE VEIL COMPLETES THE LOOK.

Headbands: The easiest type of headpiece to wear, a headband will highlight your eyes and cheekbones by pulling your hair away from your face, and it works easily with veiling. Again, the options range from plain white satin to beaded or pearled styles, colored or jeweled pieces, and wide or thin bands, depending on your taste and the thickness of your hair. They can be worn with long or short tresses.

Sculpted headpieces: Many headpiece manufacturers create pieces out of sturdy plastics, often decorated with crystals, rhinestones, silk, beads, sequins, and other appliqués. They are frequently built onto a comb or headband. Backpieces are designed to attach to the crown of your head, making it easy to add veiling (they work especially well on short-haired brides, who usually don't wear any hair

(continued on page 26)

HAND-FASHIONED METAL IS
COMBINED WITH RHINESTONES
AND PEARLS TO CREATE A
WONDERFULLY UNIQUE HEAD-
PIECE. THIS DELICATE SILVER
TIARA WORKS EXCEPTIONALLY
WELL WITH SHORT HAIR.

LOOKING FOR SOMETHING
BLUE? YOU'VE FOUND IT IN
THIS LEAFY-LOOKING, POWDER-
BLUE RHINESTONE HEADPIECE,
WHICH COULD BE WORN
ALMOST LIKE A BARRETTE
TO PULL HAIR BACK FROM
THE FACE, OR LIKE THIS, AT
THE CROWN OF THE HEAD,
ATTACHED TO A BILLOWING
FOUNTAIN VEIL.

HERE'S A TIARA FIT FOR
A QUEEN—OR FOR A ROYALLY
BEAUTIFUL BRIDE. THIS ELABO-
RATE RHINESTONE COMB IS A
SUBTLE INTERPRETATION OF
THE TRADITIONAL CROWN,
AND IS EASY TO SECURE FIRMLY
TO YOUR HAIR.

ornaments). The manufacturer of your dress may even have created a headpiece that matches it, using similar fabrics and appliqués.

Barrettes, ponytail bands, or combs: If you opt for no veil, you can pull long hair back in a single barrette or put it in a pretty ponytail with a satin- or silk-covered elastic band or a jeweled clip. Many barrettes and combs are armed with Velcro, to which veiling can be attached and then easily removed later on if you so

desire. Short cuts look great with a few strands pulled to the side with a mini jeweled barrette.

Hats: If you can't find a headpiece style you feel comfortable with, consider a hat. Go with a pillbox, à la Jackie Kennedy, or consider a romantic, wide-rimmed hat for a summer wedding. You can attach veiling, or even wrap a generous swath of tulle around the rim. Veiling is usually made from organza, tulle, or lace and comes in different lengths, styles, and even colors. You might choose a veil edged

(continued on page 30)

THIS OTHERWISE CLASSICALLY DESIGNED RHINESTONE HEADPIECE IS FASHIONED INTO SUBTLE HEART SHAPES, PERFECT FOR THE MOST ROMANTIC DAY OF A WOMAN'S LIFE. IT RESEMBLES A CROWN, BUT IT'S FAR FROM OSTENTATIOUS.

RIGHT: NEW YORK DESIGNER SUSAN HOXIE CREATES STUNNING CROWNS AND TIARAS INSPIRED BY STYLES OF CENTURIES PAST. THIS SIMPLE YET OH-SO-SPECIAL HEADPIECE INCLUDES RHINE-STONES, PEARLS, AND OTHER BEADS IN A FLORAL PATTERN.

OPPOSITE: WHAT SAYS "BRIDE" MORE THAN LAYERS AND LAYERS OF TULLE OR ORGANZA FLOATING ON THE WIND? SOME WOMEN CONSIDER THE TRADITION OF THE VEIL OUTDATED, BUT OTHERS MIGHT FIND THE IDEA OF WEARING SUCH A HEADPIECE APPEALING BECAUSE IT CONNECTS THEM TO GENERATIONS OF WOMEN.

with ribbon or satin, or something sprinkled with pretty appliqués—pearls, crystals, lace, colored petals, even butterfly shapes. Veiling can be sewn onto the headpiece, or attached separately to a comb or Velcro strip, so that it may be removed after the ceremony.

Along with a headpiece, many brides wear veils. The length and style of the veil chosen will influence not only the headpiece, but the bride's entire look. Following are some of the most popular veil types:

Blusher: A short veil worn over your face, a blusher usually hits just at or below the chin. This is a great choice for a demure, yet unfussy look.

Fly-away: With layers of veiling that brush your shoulders, a fly-away veil looks lovely and offers a hint of romance.

Fingertip: Probably the most popular length, the fingertip veil extends down to the ends of your hands, a flattering and classic style.

Waterfall: A waterfall veil is made of layers of veiling that cascade down from the top of your head like a fountain. The length of a waterfall veil varies from shoulder-length to floor-length, and is a more dramatic choice.

Mantilla: An elaborate lace veil usually worn without a headpiece, a mantilla cascades down the shoulders and back in a single or double layer, evoking a feeling of old world romance.

Waltz/Ballet: A lush, opulent look, this is floor-length veiling, often worn with a simple dress that has no train.

It's important that the veil and headpiece you choose look appropriate with, and flatter the style of, your dress. If your gown is relatively unadorned, you may

(continued on page 35)

FLOWERS ARE DEFINITELY
THE DECORATION OF CHOICE
WHEN IT COMES TO BRIDAL
HEADPIECES, AND EVEN BLOOMS
AND SPRAYS MADE OUT OF
PLASTIC AND OTHER FINE
MOLDED MATERIALS WILL
LOOK GENUINELY CHARMING.
THESE TINY BUDS ECHO THE
MINIATURE SATIN ROSES
EMBELLISHING A RING
BEARER'S PILLOW.

RIGHT: SATIN OR SILK BAND-
ING CREATES TEXTURE AND
DIMENSION ON AN OTHERWISE
UNADORNED LENGTH OF
ORGANZA. IF YOUR DRESS
HAS SPECIAL FEATURES ON
THE HEM, SLEEVES, OR WAIST,
THINK ABOUT A VEIL ACCENTED
WITH A SIMILAR PATTERN.

A CROWN OF SATIN ROSETTES
FROM JANE WILSON MARQUIS
CREATES ADDED DIMENSION
SET ATOP A MANE OF LONG,
THICK HAIR.

SILK, SATIN, TULLE, AND BEADS
EVERYWHERE. THIS WATERFALL
VEIL LOOKS LIKE A BENEVOLENT
GHOST WAITING PATIENTLY
NEXT TO AN ELABORATE
WEDDING GOWN, READY
TO ADD ROMANCE TO SOME
LUCKY BRIDE'S WEDDING DAY.

want a more ornate headpiece. On the other hand, if you opt for a full, appliquéd ball gown, you probably won't want to overwhelm it with a complicated headpiece and veil. Does your dress have gorgeous back details? Then don't wear a very long or full veil that will cover them up!

Once you make your final decision, you'll want to take your veil and headpiece along on a visit to your hairstylist to experiment with styles for your wedding day. It used to be that a bride's headpiece was literally built into her hair for the wedding; these days, with simpler headpiece options and more relaxed hairstyles, your choices are much more flexible. But you'll still want to plan it out in advance. If you want to try a new color or cut, try to make the change about six months before your wedding, so you'll have time to get used to it (or decide against it!).

A LENGTH OF TULLE AND ITS MATCHING FLYAWAY VEIL AND HEADPIECE (ON THE CHAIR, AT RIGHT) ARE SET FOR THE WEDDING DAY. KEEP YOUR VEIL SUSPENDED OR SPREAD OUT UNTIL YOU'RE READY TO DRESS. CRUSHING IT IN A BOX OR DRAWER FOR TOO LONG WILL WRINKLE THE FRAGILE FABRIC.

A HEADBAND OF LUSH ROSES
UNDER LAYERS AND LAYERS
OF TULLE CREATES A MISTY,
DRAMATIC LOOK. YOU CAN
WEAR AS MUCH OR AS LITTLE
VEILING AS YOU LIKE; THIS
BRIDE MAY CHOOSE TO WEAR
HERS FOR THE CEREMONY
ONLY, THEN REMOVE IT FOR
THE RECEPTION, WHERE
SHE'LL STILL BE CROWNED
IN FRESH FLOWERS.

ATTACHING YOUR VEILING TO
YOUR HAIR AND HEADPIECE
CAN BE QUITE A COMPLICATED
AFFAIR. DON'T SECURE IT
UNTIL THE LAST POSSIBLE
MINUTE; ASK FOR HELP FROM
YOUR BRIDESMAIDS, YOUR
HAIRSTYLIST, OR YOUR MOM,
MAKING SURE NOT TO LET
THE VEIL BRUSH AGAINST
YOUR MADE-UP FACE.

OPPOSITE: VEILS (AND NOT JUST THE "FLYAWAY" STYLE) HAVE BEEN KNOWN TO BILLOW IN THE WIND AND HIDE MORE THAN JUST THE BRIDE'S FACE ON A WEDDING DAY. BUT THEY CERTAINLY CAN MAKE FOR ROMANTIC PICTURES—AND ROMANTIC MOMENTS.

LEFT: A TINY PEARL-STUDDED HEADPIECE UNDER A SPRAY OF TULLE PERFECTLY ACCENTS THE PEARLS EMBELLISHING THIS HAPPY BRIDE'S OFF-THE-SHOULDER WEDDING GOWN.

CHAPTER TWO

GLOVES, WRAPS, AND JEWELRY

PAGE 40: OPERA-LENGTH GLOVES, PAIRED WITH A SLEEVELESS OR SHORT-SLEEVED DRESS, ADD UP TO AN ELEGANT LOOK.

OPPOSITE: THE UNADORNED BEAUTY OF THIS BRIDE'S STUNNING GOWN IS PERFECTLY COMPLEMENTED BY HER STRIKING YET SIMPLE OPERA-LENGTH GLOVES. A REGAL TIARA GIVES THE ELEGANT ENSEMBLE A TOUCH OF SPARKLE.

LEFT: DOES YOUR DRESS FEATURE PRETTY CLOTH-COVERED BUTTONS DOWN THE BACK? CONSIDER WEARING GLOVES WITH THE SAME ORNAMENTATION. THIS IVORY-COLORED PAIR ALSO FEATURES BANDS OF FABRIC AT THE CUFFS, WHICH MIGHT ALSO ECHO YOUR DRESS. IN ADDITION TO THE VEIL, GLOVES OFFER AN OPPORTUNITY TO PLAY UP THE UNIQUE DETAILS OF YOUR GOWN.

*D*uring the Victorian era, gloves were worn at each and every social event; they became popular again for special occasions in 1930s and 1940s. A return to '40s-era glamour has made gloves the rage for brides today. If you like the look, just be sure to choose the right style glove for your dress. If your gown has short sleeves, opt for wrist-length gloves; elbow-length gloves can be worn with barely-there cap sleeves. Over-the-elbow gloves look best with sleeveless or strapless dresses. If you're petite, short gloves will look best on you.

A TRIPLE STRING OF PEARLS MAY NOT SOUND LIKE IT WOULD MATCH THE SEQUINY SPARKLE OF THIS PAIR OF PUMPS, BUT THE TWO CLEARLY GO TOGETHER AS IF THEY WERE MADE FOR EACH OTHER. BLEND YOUR FAVORITE LOOKS AND YOU MAY SURPRISE YOURSELF.

For fabric, silk, silk charmeuse, and even cotton are great for warm-weather weddings; go with a heavier satin in fall and winter. Styles vary, too: you may like the simple elegance of a classic, plain style, or you may want to opt for gloves with a decorative band, buttons, or even appliqués to match your gown. Most gloves are white or ivory; let the color of your dress dictate the hue of your gloves.

A DIAMOND-ENCRUSTED DRESS WATCH IS A TRADITIONAL AND BEAUTIFUL WAY TO DRESS UP YOUR WRIST. IT MIGHT BE AN ANTIQUE INHERITED FROM A BELOVED GRANDMOTHER, OR A GIFT FROM YOUR GROOM.

OPPOSTIE: THIS PRETTY CROCHETED SWEATER CERTAINLY MAKES A LOVELY CHAIR DECORATION AT A SUNNY OUTDOOR WEDDING, BUT IT'S ALSO PERFECT TO WEAR OVER A STRAPLESS OR SLEEVELESS DRESS DURING THE CEREMONY OR TO DRAPE AROUND YOURSELF WHEN THE SUN GOES DOWN.

LEFT: MANY WEDDING GOWNS COME WITH MATCHING STOLES OR SHAWLS. THEY CAN BE AS SIMPLE AS A LENGTH OF ORGANZA BANDED WITH FABRIC THAT MATCHES THE DRESS, LIKE THIS BRIDE'S ELEGANT WRAP. YOU CAN TOSS IT OVER YOUR ELBOWS, AS SHE HAS HERE, OR YOU MAY HANG IT OVER YOUR SHOULDERS OR DRAPE IT AROUND YOUR NECK FOR DIFFERENT LOOKS.

What to do with gloves during the ring ceremony, and at the reception? Bridal gloves are designed with a small slit in the left ring finger, so you won't have to remove the gloves during the ceremony. At the reception, you'll want to remove your gloves in the receiving line or anytime you're eating or drinking during the party.

If you will wed in cool weather, or in a church that requires you to cover your shoulders, consider a wrap. Some gowns—especially strapless or sleeveless styles—

TALK ABOUT DETAILS! THESE GORGEOUS EARRINGS INCLUDE PEARLS, SPARKLING STONES, AND ELABORATE METAL WORK. JEWELS LIKE THIS DEFINITELY SHOULD NOT BE HIDDEN, AND WORK BEST WHEN HAIR IS PULLED BACK OR UP.

come complete with matching shawls or lace overlays. A cape—in satin, silk, or velvet, in bridal white or a variety of colors—can be stunning for a winter wedding; many are available with faux-fur borders. Or consider a bridal overcoat or jacket (many are made with pretty jeweled buttons) to keep yourself warm on a chilly wedding day.

A PRETTY PENDANT LOOKS
WONDERFUL FRAMED BY
ELEGANT COLLARBONES
AND THE NECKLINE OF YOUR
DRESS. CHANCES ARE YOU
CAN FIND ONE THAT FULLY
FITS YOUR PERSONAL STYLE.
THIS ORNATELY CARVED
PIECE—IT LOOKS SLIGHTLY
MEDIEVAL—FEATURES A CENTER
PEARL AND A PEARL CHAIN.

Your engagement ring and wedding band are the most important baubles you'll wear on your wedding day, but depending on the style of your dress you may also want to wear a necklace, earrings, and perhaps even a bracelet with special meaning for you (a charm bracelet, for instance). Jewelry is a wonderfully subtle way to introduce some color into your wedding outfit if you're not the type to add a dramatic splash with gloves or a vibrant wrap. Consider a sapphire

(continued on page 53)

RIGHT: THESE SILVER
RHINESTONE AND CREAMY
PEARL EARRINGS LOOK AS
THOUGH THEY COULD BE
DECORATIONS ON A PAIR
OF WEDDING-DAY STRAPPY
SANDALS. THE JEWELS OFFER
JUST THE RIGHT COMBINATION
OF CLASSIC AND MODERN;
THEY'D BE EQUALLY PERFECT
WITH AN EMBROIDERED
BALLGOWN OR A MINIMALIST
SHEATH.

OPPOSITE: THE ROSES THAT
LINE THIS BRIDE'S DÉCOLLETAGE
DON'T CALL FOR MUCH
ORNAMENTATION AROUND
HER NECK, BUT SHE HAS
COMPLEMENTED THE LOOK
NICELY WITH SHIMMERY
RHINESTONE AND PEARL
DANGLING EARRINGS.

PAGE 52: THIS SPARKLING
NECKLACE CAN LIGHT UP
THE NIGHT AT AN EVENING
WEDDING. IT WOULD LOOK
BEAUTIFUL WITH A LOW
NECKLINE—PERHAPS A
SCOOP, SQUARE, OR OFF-
THE-SHOULDER STYLE.
PAIR IT WITH A GOWN
FULL OF ITS OWN SPARKLE,
OR WEAR IT WITH A SIMPLE,
UNADORNED DRESS AND
SPOTLIGHT YOUR JEWELS.

pendant or a necklace made of multicolored crystals. Of course, the classic wedding necklace is a string of pearls—from choker to rope styles—worn with matching earrings. Ask your grandmother if you can wear her vintage clip-ons. Or simply wear the silver floating-heart necklace your fiancé gave you for your birthday, the one you never take off.

THESE DELICATE SILVER, RHINESTONE, AND PEARL EARRINGS WOULD LOOK ABSOLUTELY ELEGANT ON ANY EAR. THEY ARE LONG ENOUGH TO BE SEEN, EVEN WITH LONG HAIR.

OPPOSITE: A CHARMING
BUTTERFLY ADDS SPARKLE
AND A LITTLE "SOMETHING
BLUE" TO A SPRING WEDDING
ENSEMBLE. TINY PIECES
OF HAIR JEWELRY OFFER
ORNAMENTATION WITHOUT
THE DRAMA OF A VEIL.

LEFT: SPRING INTO MARRIAGE
WITH GARDEN-READY PEARL
BUTTON EARRINGS WITH
PRETTY RHINESTONE PETALS.
THEY'D LOOK GREAT WITH
ANY STRING OF PEARLS OR
BEADS—QUINTESSENTIAL WHITE
OR IVORY, EVEN PASTEL SHADES
OF PINK OR PURPLE—AND
THEY'LL ALSO COMPLEMENT
YOUR BOUQUET.

CHAPTER THREE

LINGERIE

PAGE 56: THIS UNIQUE GARTER IS MADE OF BUTTER-YELLOW CHIFFON, TOTALLY COMFORTABLE AGAINST YOUR THIGH, WITH JUST A BIT OF GATHERED BLUE-SATIN RIBBON AND A PRETTY BOW IN FRONT. IT'S THE PERFECT, TRADITIONAL "SOMETHING BLUE."

OPPOSITE: YOUR WEDDING DAY IS A PERFECT TIME TO TRY WEARING GARTERS AND STOCKINGS, EVEN IF YOU'VE NEVER WORN THEM BEFORE (THOUGH YOU MAY WANT TO PRACTICE FIRST). JUST BE SURE YOU KNOW HOW TO CLIP EVERYTHING TOGETHER, AND THAT THERE'S ENOUGH ROOM IN THE WAIST OF YOUR DRESS SO THAT THE GARTER BELT DOESN'T SHOW THROUGH.

LEFT: A CRINOLINE—AN UNDERSKIRT USUALLY MADE OF LAYERS OF TULLE OR NETTING, OFTEN WITH WIRING IN THE HEM TO GIVE IT ITS SHAPE—IS WORN UNDER A BALL GOWN SKIRT TO ENHANCE ITS ROMANTIC FULLNESS. MANY BRIDES FIND CRINO-LINES FUN TO WEAR BECAUSE OF THE ADDED FLOUNCINESS.

Your lingerie is the foundation upon which your flawless wedding-day look is built. Depending on your dress, you may need very specific pieces. And since this is a super-special occasion, you'll probably want them to be pretty, too. That's not to say you should sacrifice comfort—you're going to be dancing, hugging and kissing your guests, and posing for pictures for hours, and you won't want to be distracted by uncomfortable or itchy underthings. The perfect wedding-day lingerie is simple and glamorous but not too frilly—you don't want it to show through your gown!

(continued on page 63)

RIGHT: THIS PRETTY CRINOLINE HAS A SLIGHT BORDER OF LACE AT THE HEM, ALL THE BETTER TO LOOK LOVELY WHEN PEEKING OUT FROM UNDERNEATH THE SKIRT OF A WEDDING GOWN. SOME UNDERSKIRTS COME IN SUBTLE SHADES OF LAVENDER, CELADON, OR BABY BLUE, OFFERING JUST A HINT OF HUE TO A WHITE DRESS.

OPOSITE: A BUSTIER CAN GIVE ADDED SUPPORT UNDERNEATH A STRAPLESS BODICE—JUST BE SURE THE BACK IS LOW ENOUGH SO AS NOT TO SHOW AND THAT THE UNDERWIRES AND BONING ARE COMFORTABLE. (TRY THE BUSTIER ON WITH YOUR GOWN WELL BEFORE THE WEDDING DAY TO BE SURE IT DOESN'T SHOW THROUGH THE DRESS FABRIC, EITHER.) THIS ONE FEATURES A PRETTY FLORAL LACE DESIGN.

OPPOSITE: HERE'S A SUPER-
TRADITIONAL LACY GARTER
WITH A PRETTY SILK ROSE
EMBLAZONED ON THE FRONT.
WEAR YOUR GARTER JUST
ABOVE YOUR KNEE, ON THE
LEG WHERE IT FEELS MOST
COMFORTABLE. SOME BRIDES
CHOOSE TO DON AN HEIR-
LOOM GARTER, PERHAPS
THE ONE THEIR MOTHER
OR GRANDMOTHER WORE
AT HER WEDDING.

LEFT: IF YOU'RE WEARING A
PERIOD DRESS, YOU MIGHT
CONSIDER PUTTING ON A
PRETTY CORSET UNDERNEATH.
THIS ONE, FROM LE CORSET
BY SELIMA, IS MADE OF CLASSIC
LACE WITH RIBBON LACING.
JUST BE SURE NOT TO TIE
YOURSELF INTO IT TOO
TIGHTLY (GET A BRIDESMAID
OR YOUR MOM TO HELP).
AGAIN, TRY IT ON UNDER
YOUR DRESS BEFORE THE
BIG DAY.

Bra: This is your most important consideration. If your dress is long-sleeved and/or fashioned like a T-shirt in front, you may be able to wear a basic style. But many strapless, sleeveless, or low-necked gowns require a strapless bra or bustier. If your dress has a sheer or low back, you may need a bra with a special low back that won't show. Many bridal salons sell suitable styles, but you may also want to check out your favorite brand of everyday bras, to see if the line includes something that would be appropriate with your wedding dress. Be sure the bra you choose gives you enough support and doesn't poke you with sharp underwires.

Panties: Choose a comfortable, simple pair that fits you well. If your dress is close-fitting, you might want to go with a pantyhose/underwear combination

(continued on page 66)

This beautiful bustier features lacy cups and ribbon lacing. The solid fabric won't show through your gown, although the lace cups might peek out the top of a low neckline— but that's great for making you feel extra flirty, pretty, and romantic!

THIS SATIN BUSTIER IS SO
GORGEOUS IT COULD ALMOST
BE WORN AS THE BODICE OF A
STUNNING STRAPLESS GOWN.
THINK OF YOUR UNDERTHINGS
AS INTEGRAL PARTS OF YOUR
WEDDING-DAY OUTFIT; THE
TRUTH IS, THEY WORK BEHIND
THE SCENES TO MAKE YOUR
DRESS LOOK AS INCREDIBLE
AS IT DOES.

LAYERS AND LAYERS OF
TULLE CRINOLINE LOOK
FEMININE AND ROMANTIC,
AND OBVIOUSLY MAKE FOR
GREAT PHOTO OPS! THIS BRIDE
HAS CHOSEN A BALLET-SLIPPER
STYLE SHOE TO GO WITH
HER FULL SKIRTS.

garment. Or consider thong panties—but only if you've worn them before and are used to their fit!

Figure-forming pieces: If you feel the need to wear a slimmer, choose a comfortable Lycra or spandex shaper or bra slip. Just be sure your dress is not so sheer that it shows through. Try the garment out before your wedding day to make sure it's something you can comfortably wear for an extended period of time.

Crinolines and petticoats: A ball gown or a dress with a full A-line skirt may necessitate a lacy petticoat or organza crinoline to help it keep its shape. Some crinolines or underskirts come in subtle pastels, which can look fabulous under a tulle or organza skirt, offering just a flash of pretty color as you waltz around the dance floor.

(continued on page 70)

AS THIS BRIDE CLEARLY UNDERSTANDS, A PRETTY, TRANSPARENT UNDERSKIRT IS NOT SOMETHING THAT NEEDS TO BE KEPT HIDDEN! IF YOU'RE WEARING A FULL BALL GOWN WITH CRINOLINES OR PETTICOATS UNDERNEATH, FEEL FREE TO FLOUNCE AROUND AT YOUR RECEPTION—IT'S YOUR CHANCE TO SHOW OFF A LITTLE.

OPPOSITE: YOUR GROOM MAY PURCHASE A SPECIAL NIGHTGOWN FOR YOU AS A GIFT, OR YOU MIGHT CHOOSE TO SHOP FOR YOUR WEDDING-NIGHT ENSEMBLE ON YOUR OWN. THIS STUNNING SAGE GREEN NEGLIGEE, WITH CREAMY LACE TRIM, BY LE CORSET, IS BOTH SEXY AND DEMURE.

LEFT: WANT TO GO TOTALLY TRADITIONAL? WEAR STOCKINGS INSTEAD OF HOSE AND PURCHASE A GARTER BELT. YOU CAN MATCH YOUR STOCKINGS TO YOUR SHOES; THIS WHITE, LACY PAIR GOES WONDERFULLY WITH SATIN PUMPS EMBELLISHED WITH BOWS. DON'T FORGET THE ALL-IMPORTANT GARTER ITSELF, WHICH YOUR GROOM CAN REMOVE AT THE RECEPTION!

RIGHT: A LACY GARTER LOOKS GREAT RIGHT NEXT TO THE EQUALLY INTRICATE TOP OF A STOCKING. THIS BRIDE HAS ALSO DONE A FABULOUS JOB OF MATCHING THE PATTERN OF HER GARTER TO THE DESIGNS ADORNING HER WEDDING DRESS. GO FOR A MATCH—OR YOU CAN CHOOSE ANOTHER STYLE COMPLETELY! IT'S YOUR SECRET UNTIL THE BIG DISPLAY.

OPPOSITE: WHEN YOU'RE POSING FOR PICTURES AT YOUR CEREMONY AND RECEPTION, CRINOLINES WILL HELP YOUR DRESS LAY JUST SO, AND ENSURE A FLAWLESS SILHOUETTE. A RIBBON EDGE GIVES THIS PETTICOAT A SPECIAL TOUCH.

Stockings, hose, and garters: Since next to no one will see your hose, a nice sheer pair of nude, ivory, or white hose in your favorite brand will probably be sufficient (buy an extra pair in case of last-minute runs). Some brides choose to wear a special pair of silk stockings or opt for thigh-high hose held up with garters. If you decide to go with a garter belt, select one that fits snugly and comfortably. If you're marrying outdoors on a hot summer day, you may choose to skip hose altogether.

Wedding-night lingerie: When it comes to what to wear for your first night together as husband and wife, priorities switch completely. Go for fabulous and elaborate! Choose the prettiest, laciest lingerie you can find—a bra and panties, teddy, slip, or nightgown that makes you feel like a goddess.

CHAPTER FOUR

SHOES AND PURSES

PAGE 72: CLASSIC PUMPS WITH
JUST A HINT OF SHIMMER LOOK
STUNNINGLY SOPHISTICATED
NEXT TO A SIMPLE SHEATH
OF ORGANZA, OR WHEN THE
BRIDE LIFTS UP HER HEM TO
DISPLAY THEM TO FAMILY AND
FRIENDS. GO FOR THE GLITZ,
BUT BE SURE YOUR SHOES
ARE COMFORTABLE—WEAR
THEM AROUND THE HOUSE
BEFORE THE BIG DAY TO
BREAK THEM IN.

OPPOSITE: THESE SIMPLE PUMPS
HAVE A DAZZLING (NOT-SO)
SECRET: BIG POUFS OF SATIN
THAT ECHO THE WEDDING
FLOWERS PERFECTLY.
ATTENTION SHOE ADDICTS!
LOOK AT YOUR WEDDING AS
A WONDERFUL FOOTWEAR
OPPORTUNITY. WHEN ELSE
WILL YOU GET TO WEAR
SUCH A FABULOUS PAIR?

LEFT: CAN'T DECIDE BETWEEN
BEJEWELED SHOES OR A MATTE
SATIN PAIR? HAVE BOTH! THE
TIPS OF THESE SANDALS LOOK
LIKE THEY'VE BEEN DIPPED IN
SEQUINS AND PEARLS. AND
WHAT'S GOING TO BE PEEKING
OUT FROM UNDERNEATH YOUR
HEM? YOUR TOES, OF COURSE!

*T*here truly are wedding shoes to match every style. Everything from strappy sandals and classic pumps to platforms and slides are available, in satin and silk and in shades of white, ivory, and cream. Slingbacks—perhaps with a flirty open toe, through which pretty polished nails can peek—are a super-romantic choice.

The sky's the limit as far as style and price (you can spend twenty-five dollars on a simple pair of dyeable shoes or upwards of four hundred dollars for designer couture shoes), but just as with lingerie, you'll want to make sure your shoes are comfortable. Don't hobble around painfully in the name of fashion on your wedding day! Since most people won't even see your shoes under your long skirt,

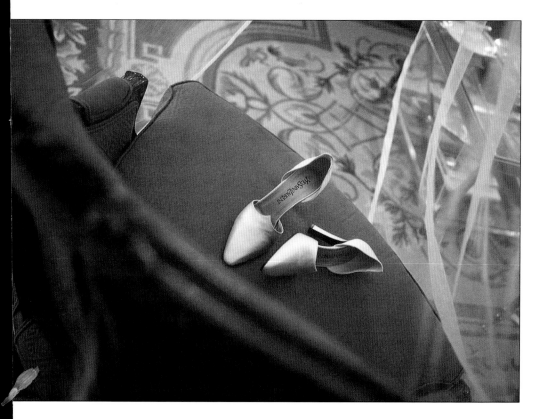

OPPOSITE: ANY MODERN
BRIDE WILL ADORE THE
UNEMBELLISHED LOOK OF
THESE PRETTY, STRAPPY
SANDALS FROM STUART
WEITZMAN. WHETHER YOU
CHOOSE A CLOSED HEEL
WITH CRISS-CROSSED STRAPS
(TOP), OR A JEWELED OPEN-
HEELED LOOK, THE DELICATE
STRAPS WILL SHOW OFF
SLENDER ANKLES.

LEFT: THESE STYLISH SHOES
ARE ELEGANT AND SEXY—
CHECK OUT THOSE HEELS!
BE SURE YOU'RE COMFORTABLE
IN THE HEEL HEIGHT YOU
SELECT. IF YOU'RE NOT A
HEELS KIND OF GIRL, YOUR
WEDDING IS DEFINITELY NOT
THE OCCASION ON WHICH TO
BECOME ONE. THINK OF THE
MOST COMFORTABLE DRESS
SHOE YOU WEAR, THEN FIND
A WEDDING PAIR.

it makes sense to wear shoes that feel good. You may even consider buying shoes a half-size larger than your regular size for maximum comfort; of course, make sure the shoes aren't so loose that they slip off your feet.

Take care to give your toes and ankles the support they deserve. By all means, choose a heel and a toe shape that you are used to wearing. Unless you are very petite, or are used to wearing very high heels, it might be best to wear a shoe with a low heel, under two inches. Consider a shoe with a chunky, square heel

(continued on page 84)

RIGHT: DESIGNER KENNETH
COLE DRESSES UP A SIMPLE
MARY JANE–STYLE SHOE
WITH TINY PEARLS AND
EMBROIDERED PETALS.
PRECIOUS DETAILS LIKE THESE
MAKE EVEN THE MOST BASIC
WHITE SHOE UNFORGETTABLE.
APPLIQUÉS ARE ALSO A GREAT
WAY TO ADD A BIT OF COLOR
TO A WHITE SHOE.

OPPOSITE: ADD SOME SHINE
TO YOUR SHOE STYLE BY
CHOOSING SANDALS WITH
BEJEWELED BUCKLES. IT'S
SMALL DETAILS SUCH AS
THESE THAT MAKE YOUR
ENTIRE WEDDING DAY SO
SPECIAL, FROM THE TOP
OF YOUR HEAD ALL THE
WAY DOWN TO THE TIPS OF
YOUR TOES.

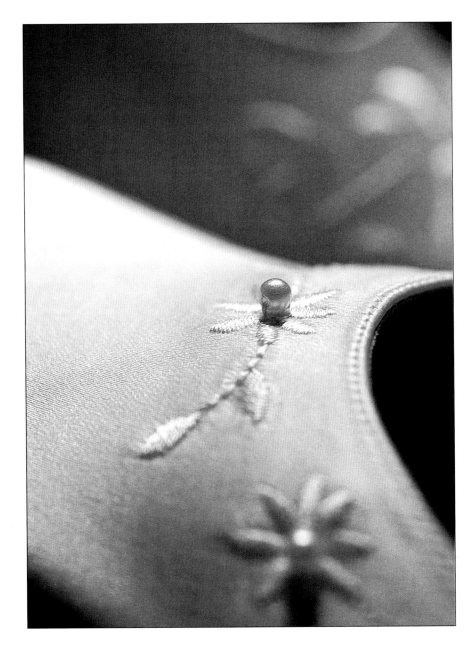

RIGHT: SLENDER STRAPS ADD A DASH OF SEXY STYLE TO THESE SHOES, WHICH WILL LOOK GREAT WITH ANY STYLE DRESS. LOTS OF ROOM FOR THE TOES SUGGESTS THAT THEY'RE COMFORTABLE, TOO.

OPPOSITE: THESE SATIN SLIPPERS RECALL ERAS LONG PAST AND PERFECTLY COMPLEMENT THE LACY ROMANCE OF A PERIOD GOWN. THEY'LL MAKE WONDERFUL HEIRLOOMS, TOO.

OPPOSITE: AS WITH JUST ABOUT EVERY OTHER PIECE OF BRIDAL CLOTHING, FLORAL ACCENTS ARE WILDLY POPULAR WHEN IT COMES TO WEDDING SHOES. CHOOSE SOMETHING SUITABLY SUBTLE, LIKE THIS PRETTY LEAF PATTERN, OR WEAR A PAIR DECORATED WITH PRETTY PETALS THAT GO WELL WITH YOUR DRESS.

LEFT: CAN'T GET OVER THE BEAUTY OF THE EMBROIDERY ON YOUR DRESS? SEE IF YOU CAN FIND A PAIR OF SHOES THAT ECHO IT, LIKE THIS PAIR OF PUMPS WITH THEIR SATIN-RIBBON PATTERN. CONSIDER A VEIL WITH SIMILAR SATIN BANDING TO COMPLETELY PULL TOGETHER YOUR LOOK.

RIGHT: WHO EVER SAID
YOU HAD TO MATCH YOUR
SHOES TO YOUR DRESS? THESE
JEWELED HEELS ARE A MAJOR
SURPRISE UNDER A WHITE
WEDDING GOWN. SHOES ARE
A GREAT WAY TO EXPRESS
A BIT OF PERSONALITY OR
WHIMSY, WHETHER YOU WEAR
A TRADITIONAL DRESS OR A
LITTLE WHITE WEDDING SUIT.

OPPOSITE: NOT EVERY
WEDDING PURSE IS WHITE.
THIS GOLD BAG WITH
INTRICATE BEADING WOULD
LOOK RIGHT AT HOME CLASPED
IN THE HAND OF A HAPPY
BRIDE. CHOOSE A BAG BIG
ENOUGH TO CARRY WHAT
YOU NEED AS WELL AS
ONE THAT FITS WITH YOUR
PERSONAL STYLE—ON
WEDDING DAY OR ANY DAY.

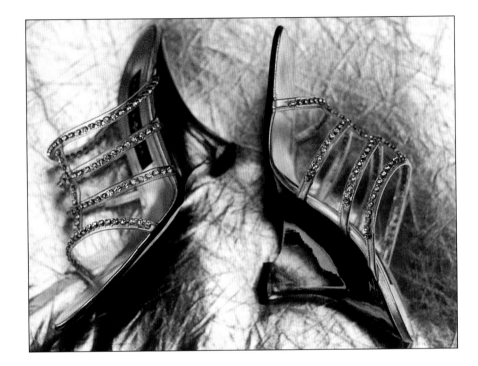

and a roomy round or square toe box, which will be much easier to walk and dance in than a pointy-toed stiletto. Some brides opt for ballet slippers or flats. If you're committed to comfort over tradition, opt for bridal sneakers decorated with pearls and ribbon ties. You may even choose two pairs—"formal" shoes for the ceremony, then a more comfortable pair for the reception. Be sure to choose your shoes (or at least decide on the heel height you'll wear) by the time of your first dress fitting so that your hem can be altered to just the right length.

You're in luck when it comes to a wedding-day purse—there are so many choices, you're sure to find the bag that suits your personality and flatters your dress.

OPPOSITE: CONSIDER MAKING YOUR OWN WEDDING PURSE—THIS ONE WAS SEWN EASILY FROM RECTANGLES OF FABRIC, WITH A BAND AND HANDLE MADE OF PLAYFUL TRIM. SILK ROSES ARE SEWN ON TO ONE SIDE, EMBELLISHED WITH ORGANZA RIBBON.

LEFT: THIS BRIDAL DRAWSTRING PURSE IS DECORATED WITH A BIT OF SWIRLY TRIM THAT ECHOES THE SHAPE OF THE BAG ALONG THE EDGES. WANT TO WEAR A PURSE YOU'LL USE AGAIN? A SIMPLE WEDDING-DAY BAG LIKE THIS CAN BE DYED ANY COLOR YOU PREFER ONCE YOU'RE A NEWLYWED.

You might choose a silk or satin bag that matches your dress down to the beaded appliqués. Or go with a raw-silk drawstring bag in any color of the rainbow. Some special-event handbags are covered with silk flowers or even made from fresh blooms by a floral designer. Some brides opt for a silk clutch in a vivid jewel tone, or a little black purse decorated with miniature rhinestones. Regardless of what sort of bag you choose, remember that it should be functional as well as beautiful. An evening bag should be big enough to hold a few necessities: a small compact, lipstick, and perhaps a bottle of clear nail polish and a sampling of perfume.

OPPOSITE: ROMANTIC, TRADI-
TIONAL BRIDES AND MODERN,
FASHION-FORWARD BRIDES
ALIKE WILL LOVE THIS SILK
POUCH, WITH ITS BEAUTIFUL
BEADED PATTERN AND STYLISH
HANDLES. DON'T FORGET TO
TUCK A HANDKERCHIEF INTO
YOUR PURSE, WHETHER FOR
SENTIMENTAL REASONS (IT
BELONGED TO YOUR GREAT-
GRANDMOTHER) OR PRACTICAL
ONES (THOSE TEARS YOU'RE
SURE TO SHED).

LEFT: THIS SOPHISTICATED
WEDDING-DAY BAG IS BOTH
PRACTICAL AND PRETTY.
IF A FRILLY OR SHINY BAG
JUST ISN'T YOU, OPT FOR
SOMETHING SIMPLE AND
FAMILIAR IN OFF-WHITE
OR IVORY.

OPPOSITE: A PRETTY SATIN DRAWSTRING HOLD-ALL IS THE PERFECT PURSE FOR A WEDDING DAY. WHAT DO YOU NEED A BAG FOR, YOU ASK? MUST-HAVES AND LAST-MINUTE EMERGENCY SUPPLIES LIKE CLEAR NAIL POLISH (FOR RUNS), BOBBY AND SAFETY PINS, A MINI BOTTLE OF HAIR SPRAY, A TINY MIRROR, LIPSTICK, AND MASCARA.

LEFT: THIS GORGEOUS PURSE, WITH ITS BRAIDED STRAP AND BASKET-WEAVE PATTERN, WOULD LOOK FABULOUS WORN WITH A DRESS WITH SIMILAR DETAILS, OR ADD TEXTURE TO A RELATIVELY UNADORNED GOWN. IT'S BIG ENOUGH TO CARRY EVERYTHING YOU NEED, BUT NOT SO HUGE THAT IT WILL FEEL LIKE A KNAPSACK.

RIGHT: THIS TINY BEADED EVENING BAG WILL DANGLE FROM YOUR WRIST LIKE A PIECE OF EXQUISITE JEWELRY. JUST BIG ENOUGH TO HOLD A LIPSTICK, COMPACT, AND PERHAPS A HANDKERCHIEF, IT'S A STYLISH WAY TO CARRY YOUR WEDDING DAY ESSENTIALS.

OPPOSITE: IF YOU CHOOSE TO WEAR GLOVES, BE SURE TO SELECT A MATCHING WEDDING-DAY BAG TO BEAUTIFULLY FINISH YOUR LOOK. THESE MATTE-SATIN GLOVES LOOK GREAT WITH A SIMPLE WHITE POUCH WITH A DRAWSTRING TOP MADE TO LOOK LIKE A DELICATE BLOOM.

Belle Fleur

11 East 22nd Street

New York, NY 10010

(212) 254-8703

Flowers

le Corset by Selima

80 Thompson Street

New York, NY 10012

(212) 334-4936

Lingerie

Jane Wilson Marquis

155 Prince Street

New York, NY 10012

(212) 477-4408

Dresses, headpieces, veils, and accessories

Kenneth Cole

New York, NY

(800) KEN COLE

www.kennethcole.com

Shoes

Lyn Hughes Photography

114 West 27th Street

New York, NY 10001

(212) 645-8417

Wedding photography

Maxine Grand Fabrics, Inc.

150 West 26th Street

New York, NY 10001

(212) 741-7454

Fabrics

S.Hoxie NEW YORK

(212) 360-7139

Headpieces

Stuart Weitzman

625 Madison Avenue

New York, NY 10022

(212)750-2555

www.stuartweitzman.com

Shoes

**TATI - The Bridal Superstore
from France**

475 Fifth Avenue

New York, NY, 10017

212-481-8284

www.tatiusa.com

Gowns, shoes, accessories, lingerie

Principal Photograpy ©Lyn Hughes: 1, 3, 8, 10, 11, 12, 13, 17, 18, 19, 20, 21, 23, 24, 25, 26, 27, 28, 31, 32, 33, 36, 38, 40, 43, 44, 45, 46, 47, 48, 49, 50, 52, 53, 54, 55, 56, 58, 59, 60, 61, 62, 63, 64, 65, 66, 67, 68, 69, 70, 71, 72, 74, 75, 76, 77, 78, 79, 80, 81, 82, 83, 84, 85, 86, 87, 88, 89, 90, 91, 92, 93

©Sarah Merians Photography & Company: 2, 6, 14, 16, 22, 29, 34, 35, 37, 39, 42, 51

ABOUT THE AUTHOR

Tracy Guth was an associate features editor at *BRIDE'S* magazine and the managing editor of The Knot (www.theknot.com) before striking out on her own as a freelance writer and editor specializing in wedding-related subjects. The author of *Dresses* and *Flowers*, two books in the For Your Wedding series, she has also written and edited for *Seventeen* and *Good Housekeeping*. Born and raised in Chicago, Tracy now lives and writes in New York City.